How to Draw Anime Fast!

By Irma Neely

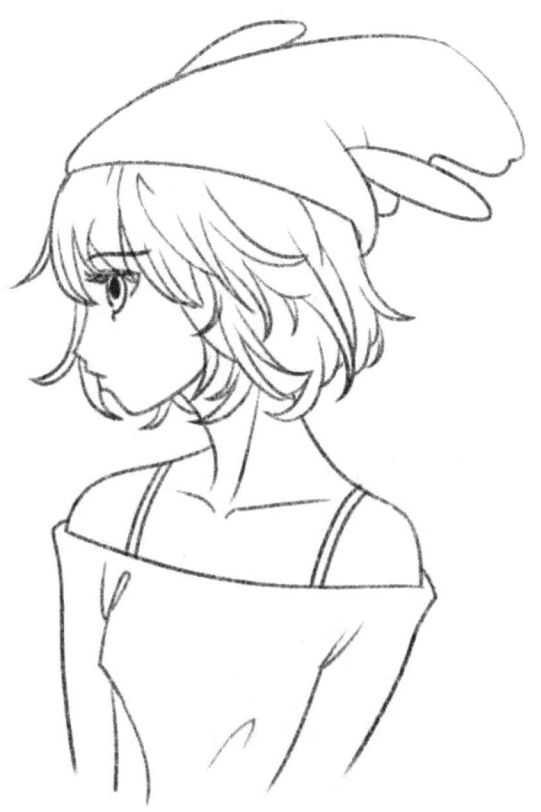

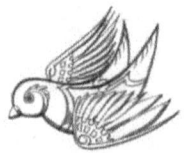

Table of contents

Introduction

Line, composition, placement, shape, form, and detail these are just some aspects of drawing that you have to concern yourself when you want to make a great looking drawing. Drawing starts with drawing what other people have drawn and then once you get the gist of how they have drawn their pictures, then you start to realize you can turn lines, shapes, forms, and details into your own creations. These anime drawings are a great addition to your repertoire of drawings and help you on your way to your own creations.

Drawing is an excellent relaxing way to spend your time. It is a quiet activity that involves you. You can also draw with your children and friends. So, although you can just as easily draw by yourself, you can get a group of people together and draw as a group. It's nice to be in the presence of other like-minded people that enjoy drawing just as you do. Drawing is a self-expression that helps person feel self-confidence, self-esteem, and a bit of happiness.

Anime is new and exciting, modern and fun. It is a great way to start drawing. This guide has seven drawings which gives you a variety of images to draw and learn from. Whether it is the anime rabbit or girl that you love, anime is a world-wide popular style. Drawing is a great way to get to know Japanese animation better. The seven drawings are pretty easy yet interesting in style. Easy sometimes has a connotation of plain, but the seven varieties of anime in this guide are chosen to stimulate your creative side.

This guide is going to walk you through step by step the process to create an interesting anime drawing.

You will learn such things as placement on the paper, how simple shapes guide you to the final product of your anime. As well, you will learn the importance of the line and not to get too attached to a line you have drawn, because you will need to erase some lines to get your final product. It is just part of the process of making a great looking picture.

The first chapter is the importance of buying the right tools. So, once you have that down, pick a nice quiet space or a busy one if you prefer. Sometimes where you draw makes a difference in how your picture is going to turn out. You might work better when there are a lot of people around and your mind natural focuses though the noise.

You could figure out that total silence is the key to your success in drawing. It takes a little investigation to figure out what is best for you. A person may sit in a big class and somehow something is making them nervous making their picture turns out shaky. No worries just try drawing in the quiet with no one around and you might do better like that. There is no right way, only that on the one makes you comfortable and the one that make you draw. Now let's start the process of drawing these great anime drawings.

Chapter 1

Preparing to draw

Drawing starts with you and your comfort. Pick a comfortable spot to draw where there are very little distractions, unless you like distractions. You want a comfortable chair that makes you want to work not sit back and sleep. You also want a nice hard surface that is clean and free from bumps.

Can use any pencil or pen to draw, but let me say that if you get a little better-quality pencil or pen it may be a bit easier to make your pictures look the way you want them to look. Zebra makes really wonderful pencils, and you can order them from the web. The drawings in this book are created with pencil and a thin tipped marker. You may use any colour you want or marker, but the tip is going to make a difference in how the marker is going to look. You may also use coloured pencils, or any type of pen you feel you want. There really is no limitation, but the way it looks will be altered by the tip of the marker. What you do need to keep in mind though is the width of the tip. The tip is too thick it can make it difficult to get a clean thick line. Drawing does not have to be obsolete. Play around a while and get to know your tools. Every artist has to learn what works best for them.

The kind of paper you choose is important too. You want to practice on cheap paper, but you don't have to. You can buy a drawing book if you want to see your progression. Paper does not cost that much money so if it inspires you to buy a nicer paper to draw on, go for it. You want to draw on paper that has no lines.

If you feel that you want to frame your drawings when they are done, then use a piece of loose paper that will fit into a frame that can easily hang on your wall.

If you go to an art store or the craft store, instead of using a pink rubber on the end of a pencil, they make a fabulous white rubber that makes the least amount of marks on your paper. You want to get a couple of those. It's easier to have the rubber off of the pencil, and the white rubbers have a larger surface so it is easier and doesn't wear down as fast. These little things make a difference so you can concentrate and make the best picture you can.

Pick a time when you are alert and feel good when you want to draw. You don't want to be tired because art can be a little frustrating at first. You are training yourself to do something. You won't be perfect at first so be in a willing mood and you are up for the best chance at success. Now that you have your tools, let us take a look at how to draw seven anime drawings.

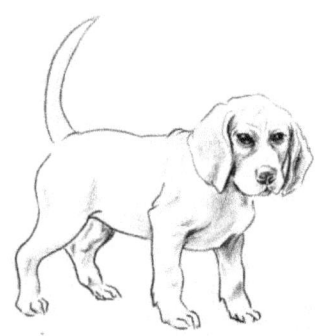

Chapter 2 – Drawing cute anime rabbit. Learn to draw basic shapes

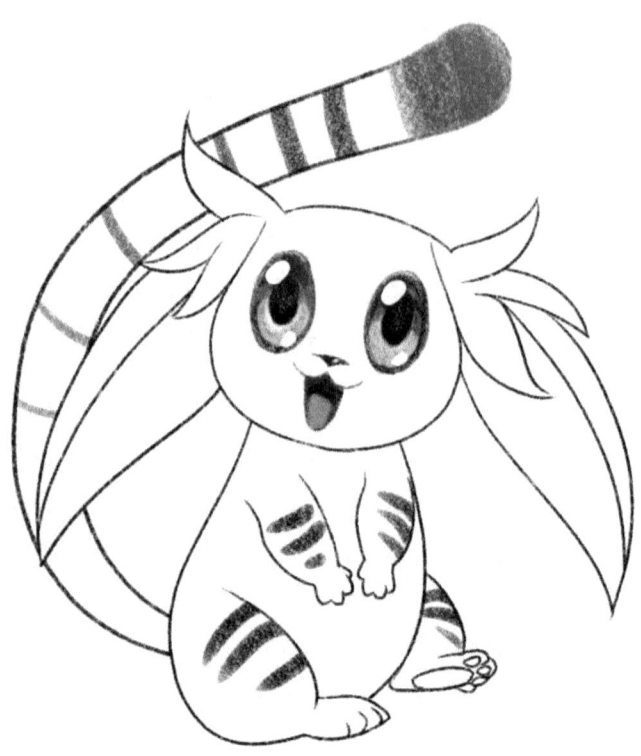

Drawing shapes

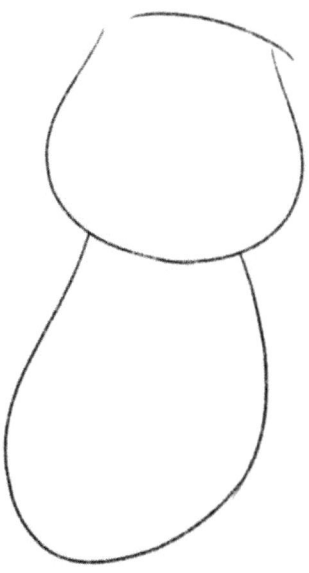

With drawing when you know where you are going it makes the picture come out a lot easier. The best way to do this is through starting with shapes. Even before you put anything down on the paper, you want to make sure you position your main subject correctly. So, you can see you start the top right corner of the rabbit's head to the left of the center line. Then you are going to build your shapes with small lines. You notice these are not describable shapes they are unique to the anime animal. Study the shapes in the book before you start drawing on your paper. Notice the subtle angles and curves that make up the shapes. Notice how the line that makes up the bottom of the rabbit's head go up not down. The subtleties are important.

Drawing face

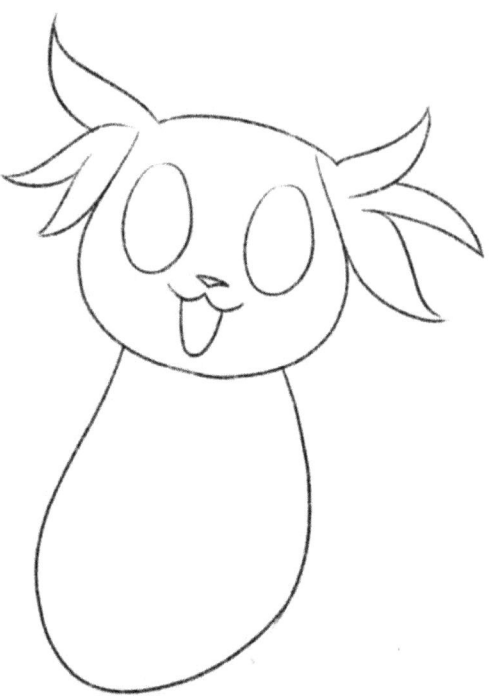

You are going to sketch in the shapes of the ears and eyes. You want to draw a subtle curve line in the middle of your first two shapes so you can tell where to position the ears, so they are symmetrical. Also add two ovals: shapes for the future eyes. Draw a mouth. With all the pictures look at the picture in the book and then at your drawing and compare the two, so they match before you move on. It helps to step back from your drawing so you can see clearly what you have done.

Drawing body

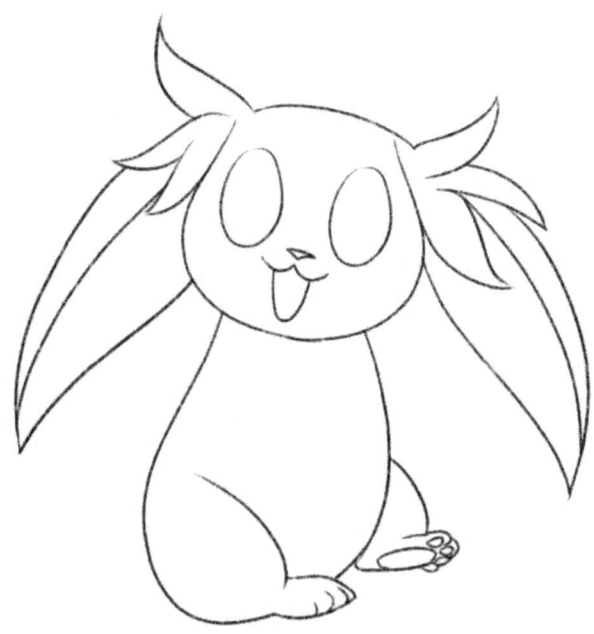

You will be putting in rabbit's face, arms, and feet. You will be erasing some of your shapes lines in order to make room for rabbit's limbs. Use the line you drew before to help place the eyes. You can slowly build them with small lines. Use the far-right line starting point to judge the placement of the rabbit's arms. Always notice the angles and the subtle curves that make up the lines of the parts of the rabbit. Very important is that small curve at the bottom that makes up the belly of rabbit. Notice the dynamics of this picture where the lines go in all different directions.

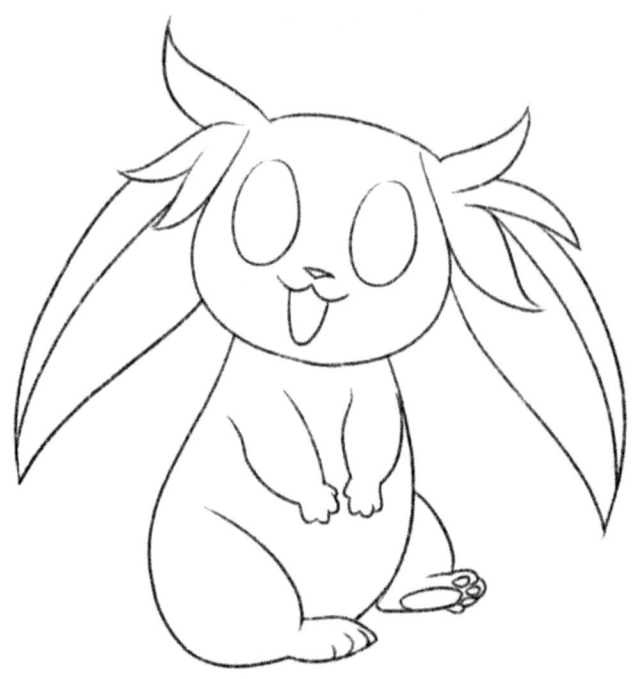

Next steps are where rabbit really takes on the anime style. You are going to draw in the detail of the eyes. The three details of the eyes make up the anime eye look. You can build them slowly with small lines to make up the proper shapes. Erase and redraw if you have to. You can work up to drawing the lines up correctly first off, the bat. There is no pressure erase as many times as you need until you get it right. Look from this picture to your picture to make sure that yours matches what is here. Do not forget the small little details of the jagged lines on the head and ears that represent the hair. This is also part of the anime style.

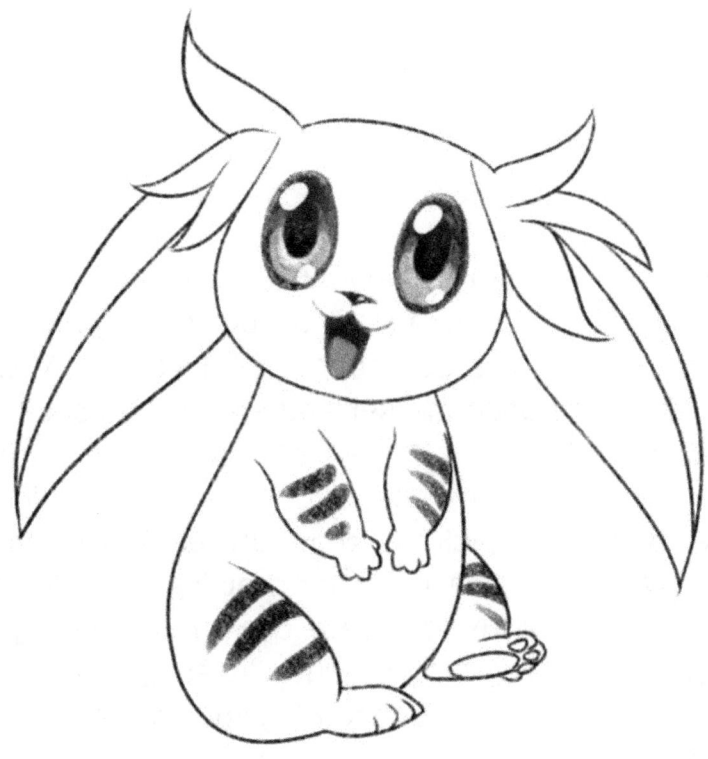

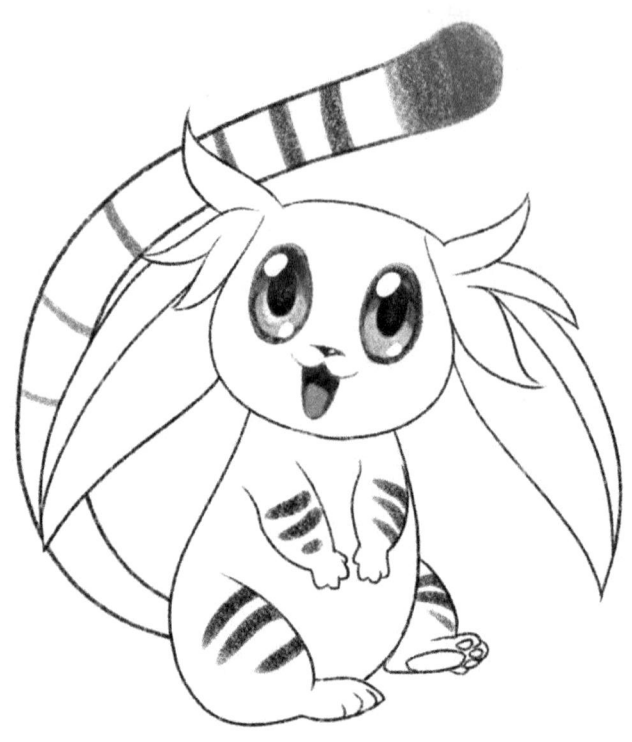

It is time for ink in this final step. Also, you can add a tail. The tail you can judge to place not too much further up from the bottom of the left side. You will take your fine tipped marker and trace the pencil lines. You want to follow as closely as you can. It can build slowly if you want by connecting small black lines to create the longer black line that you see. If you want to make longer lines remember that drawing is an illusion so you can wave slightly to create the straight line. If you look at the drawing closely you will see the very subtle wave in the line that ends creating the line that appears very neat and clean. You will fill in the eyes by drawing black lines next to each other neatly.

Chapter 3 – Anime teen: learn to draw anime body

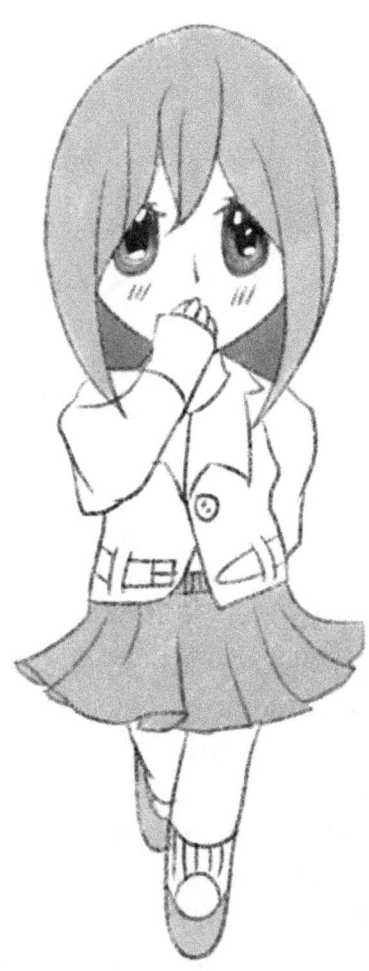

Drawing the head and hair

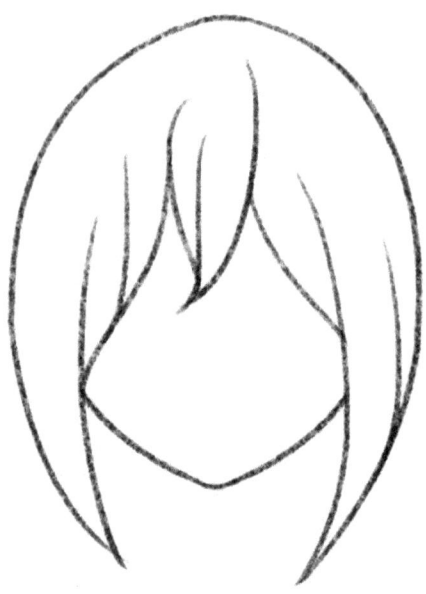

Step one for anime teen starts off the same as rabbit anime. You want to position the shapes properly on the paper. Remember you want to be slightly off center to make the illusion of straightness. Take a look at this picture well before you begin and study the lines and their angles. You will build them slowly with small lines. Take your time. Check out the angles and the curves, also the length. Look between your picture and this picture in the book to make sure everything matches. Draw in the jagged hair that makes the anime look.

Drawing body shape

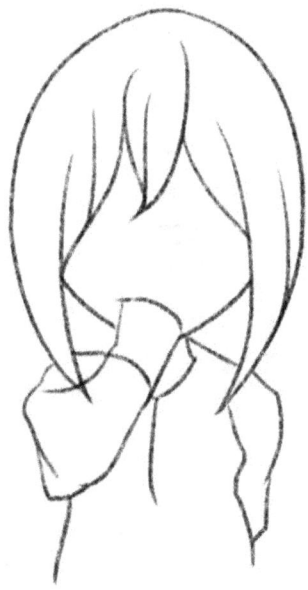

Now you are going to expand on the shapes that you have. You will be erasing lines that are normal. Study this photo and your photo and use your initial guidelines to build the arms and the definition of the body. The direction of each line is important too. You will build the image slowly. Erase as much as you need or just draw another line until it is about right.

You will also add the teen's shirt and the skirt. Check your picture against this one before moving on. Start from the top and just look back and forth to each picture to make sure the lines match closely.

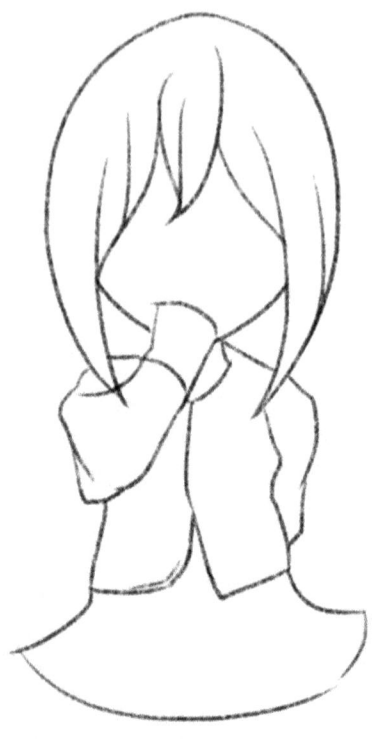

You will also add the legs and the shoes.

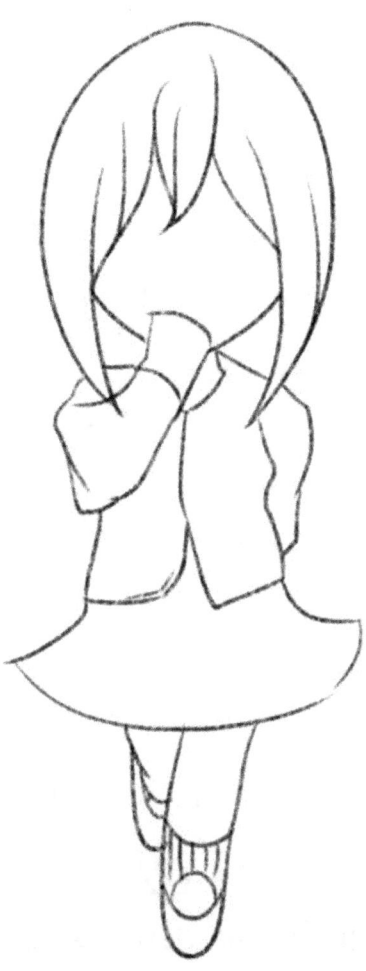

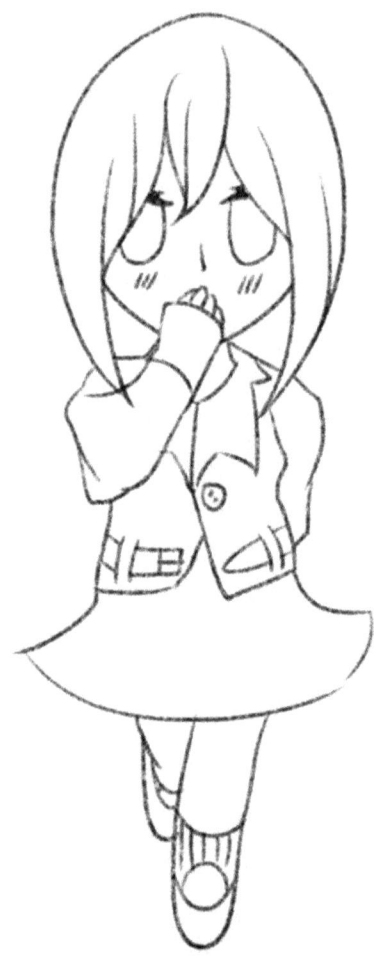

This step is all about the detail of the anime face and clothes. The small lines also make up her eyebrows and nose. As well, you will draw the detail of the teen's shirt. You will follow your pencil lines with the cleanest ink line. If you have to start over and try again it is no problem. Once, you do a few times you will get the hang of it. Go back and erase with your white rubber any lines that don't fit.

This step is about adding more detail. You will be filling in the black ink of the eyes and the skirt detail. To fill in all around the circles in the eyes, and leave the little circles white. You will put in the three circles that make up the reflections in eyes.

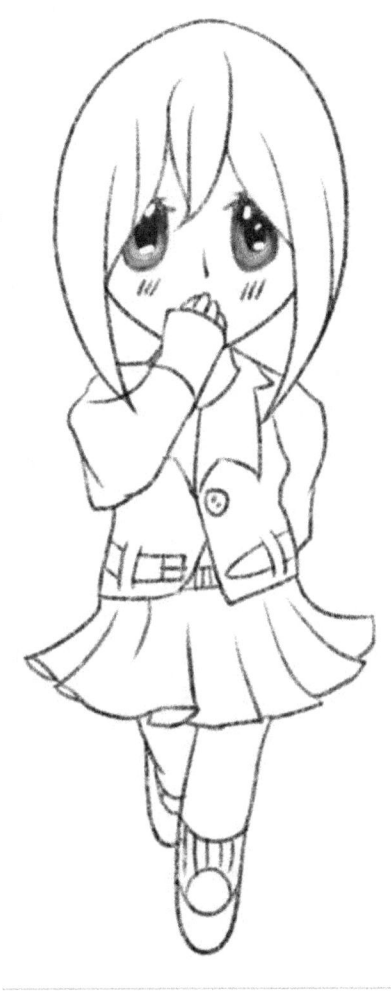

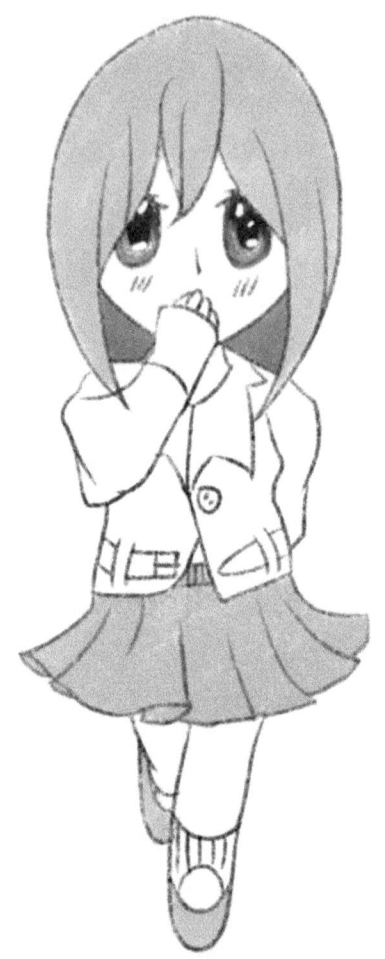

The last step is about filling in the final details that really make this teen interesting. You are going to use variations between a little coloured markers, watercolour paint, or acrylic paint to fill in the darker gray areas. You will also go over and create some very light lines for the added contrast and detail. Inspect this picture from head to toe and compare it to yours from head to toe. Just add in whatever is missing as you go. You will be looking back and forth.

Chapter 4 – Smiling anime girl: drawing anime face and emotions

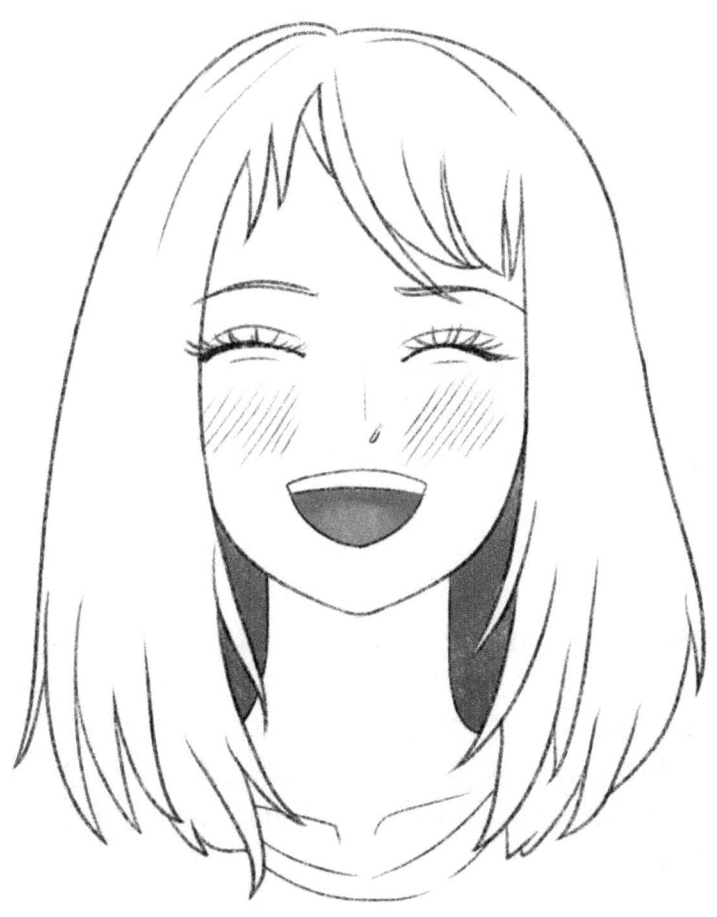

Drawing shape

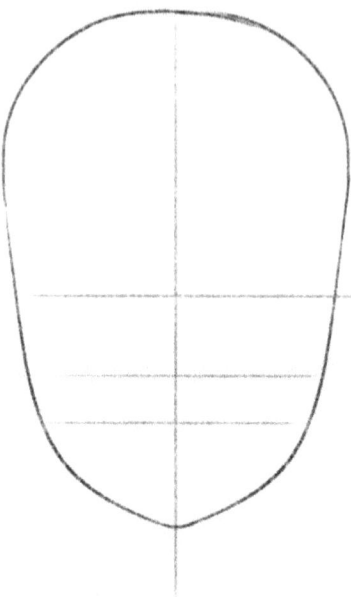

The smiling girl is a little easier than the teen. The beginning of smiling girl is about making the outlines of her face. You want the center to be slightly to the left of the actual center of the paper. Draw your symmetry line so you can position the eyes and the nose correctly, as well as the mouth.

Drawing hair

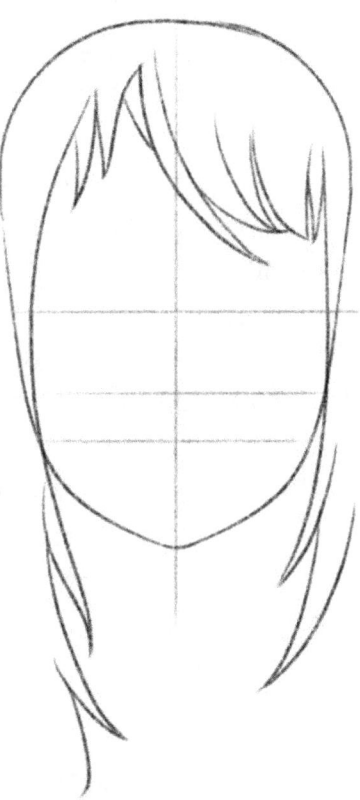

The next step is about drawing her hair. Remember you can build the lines slowly. You are making sketch lines because the end result will be inked and then you will erase what you don't use. As always study the curve of the lines. Do they curve up down, is the curve slight or large? Is it more of a slant from a horizontal line or a vertical line? Horizontal line is left to right like the horizon.

Here use the sides of the hair to guide you where to start drawing the eyes. This will help you complete the lines of the face. As you can see this picture is about long lines creating the features. Look this picture and you're drawing to match up the lines. Build the lines, small lines at a time if you have to. You can connect small little lines to create one big one. As you can see in order to match the lines that are here. See that the lines go different ways and curve in different directions. This creates the illusion. For the most part no one's hair all goes in one direction. Again, with these lines just go ahead and match this picture with your drawing. You can start left to right to match all the lines up.

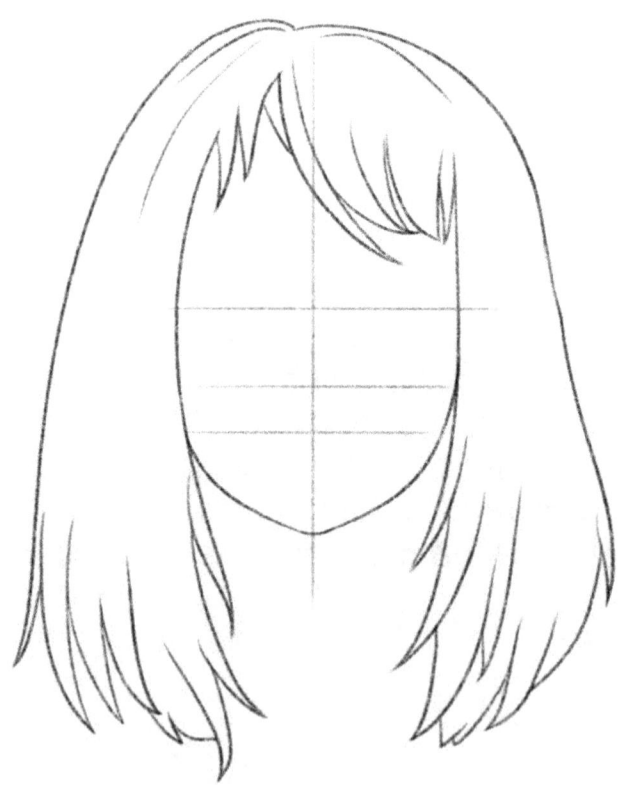

Drawing anime eyes

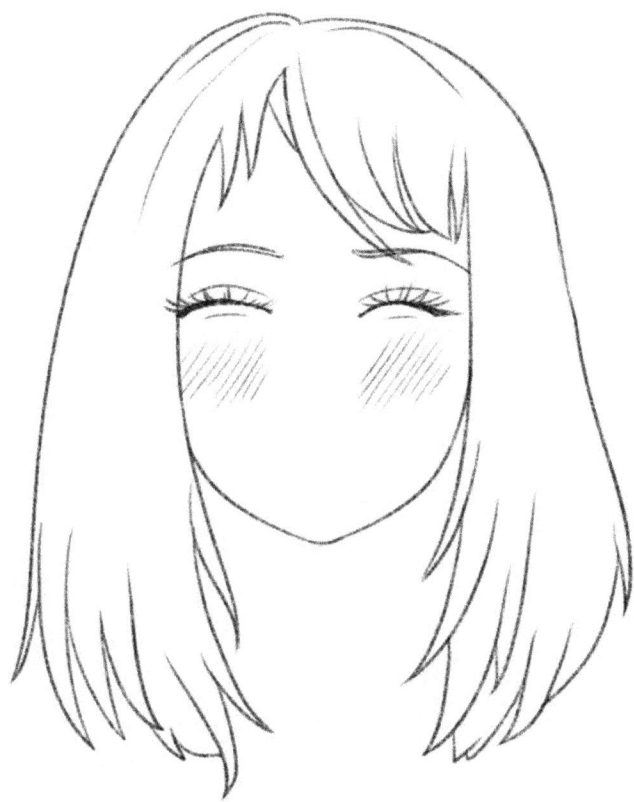

It is where you will begin really putting in the detail eyes lines. You can see the girl's eyes are closed because we draw a smiling girl. Do not forget about the eyelashes, they are long and make the girl incredibly beautiful. Eyebrows are thin and drawn by a slim line, you can use the curve shape. Add the cheeks: these are semi vertical strokes.

Then focus on the mouth and nose. The nose is neat and small, just use two simple lines.

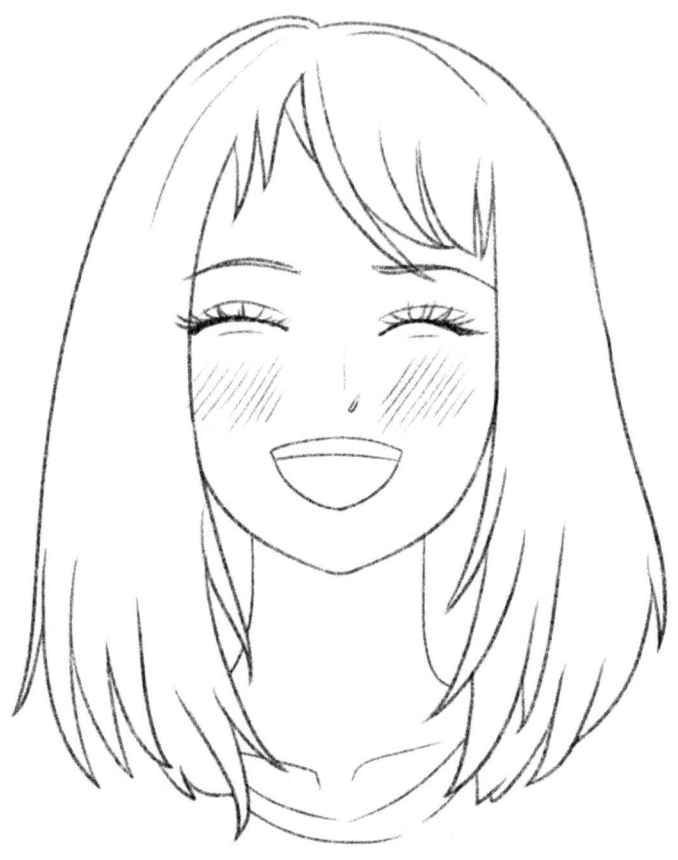

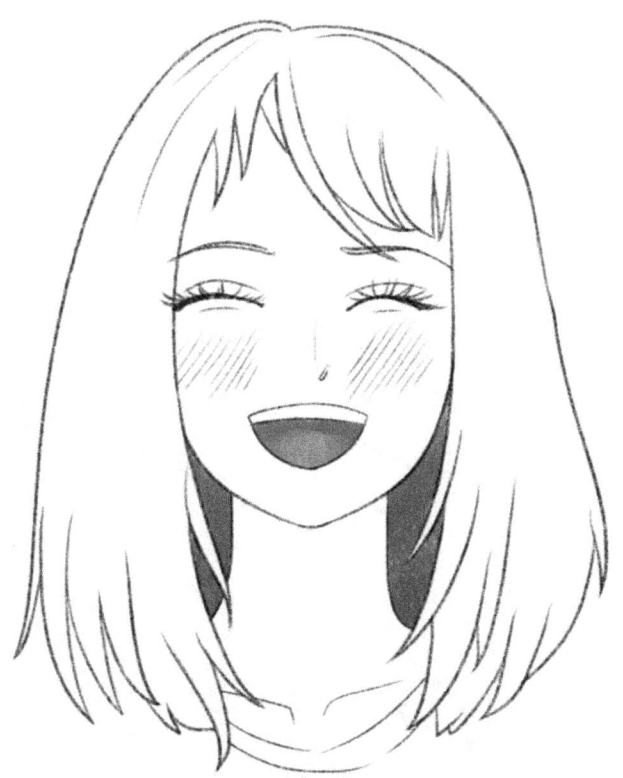

In this final you are taking your ink pen and tracing your pencil lines to bring smiling girl to life. Remember to build the long lines with short small ones. Wait until your pen ink dries before you erase the excess pencil lines. Take a look at this picture before you start so you have an idea of where you are going. You can start from the top of the head and go down or go from left to right. You want to be consistent so you don't rest your hand on the wet ink.

Chapter 5 – Drawing little kitten

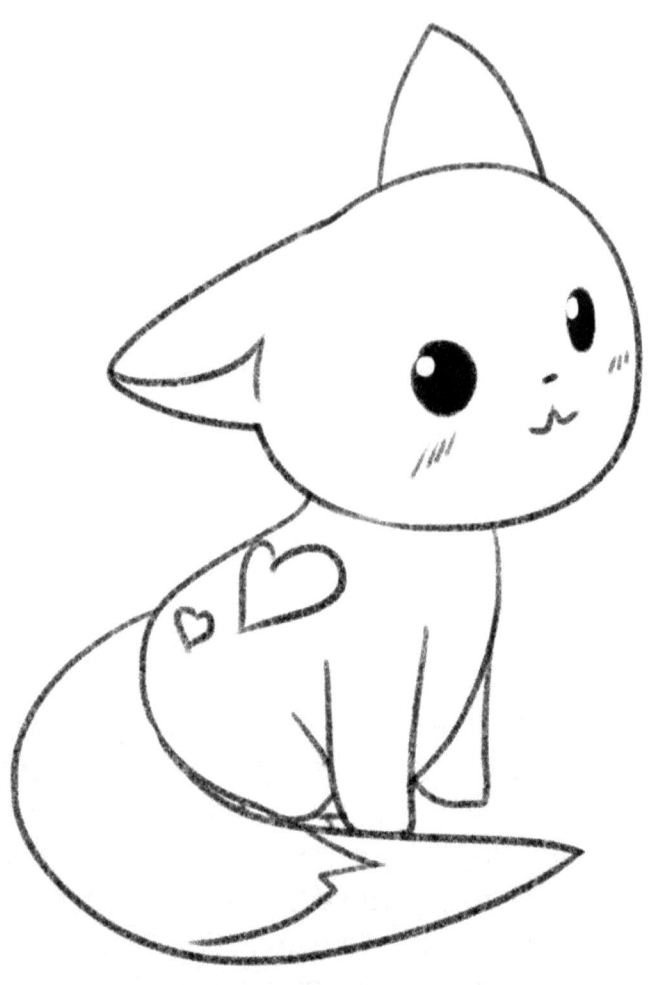

Drawing shape

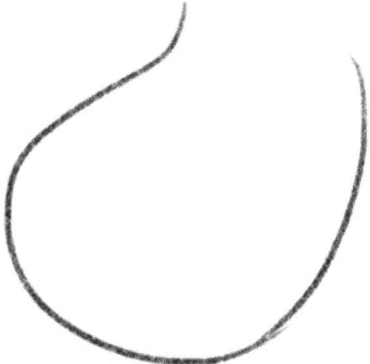

It is all about drawing the main shapes of the cat for a guideline. You draw place the body in the center of the page. Notice the shape isn't quite an egg and not quite a football. Just form it with small lines and compare. Then notice the curve on the right of the body curves in and the on the left slants down and then drops down and curves out.

Drawing face detail

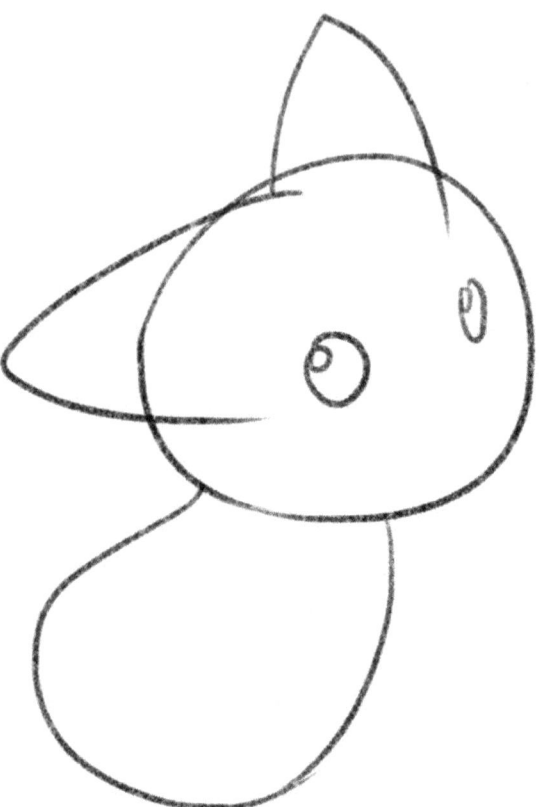

It is time to draw the kitten's head, ears and eyes. Ears are with sharp angles. The next step is creating the eyes: draw circles and small circles inside them. Small inner circles must be placed symmetrically inside.

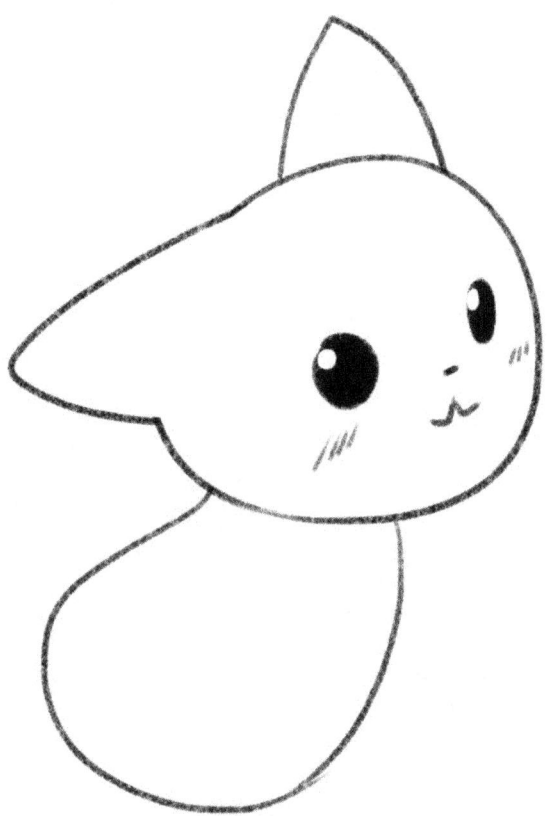

You will be smoothing things out a little. Shade eyes to fill in all around the circles in the eyes, and leave the little circles white. Add a nose, it is very small and cute.

Here you begin to draw legs, fore and hind are. Take a look at this picture and yours and make sure all the lines are similar before moving on.

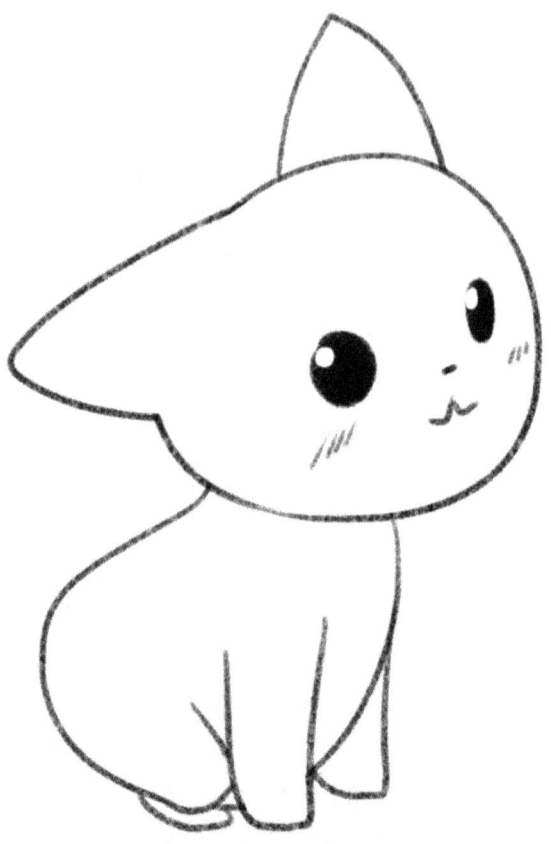

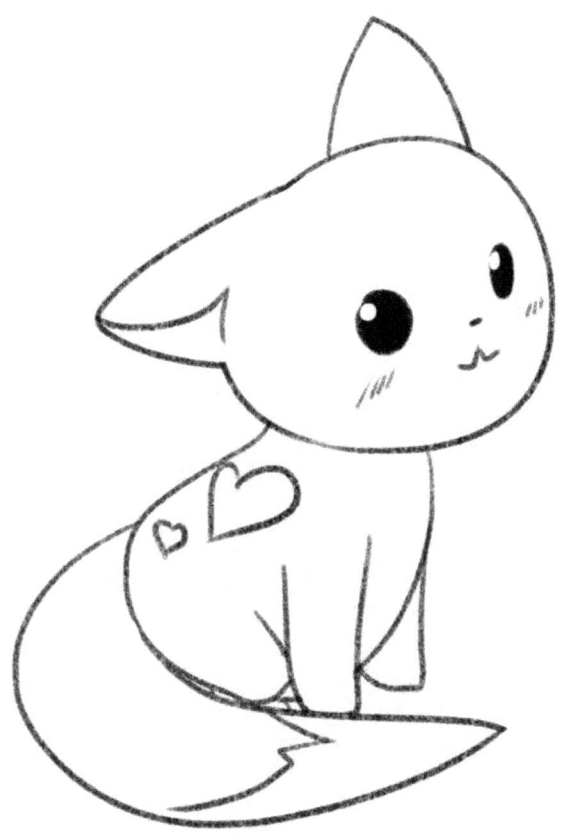

It's time to draw tail, as you can see it's exquisite and beautiful. If you want to use imagination let's draw some little hearts on the back. Compare this picture with your drawing and fill in any missing lines. This picture is pretty simple so you if you have to start over its fine. It looks very similar excellent. Let's move on.

Chapter 6 – Pretty anime girl: drawing anime face profile

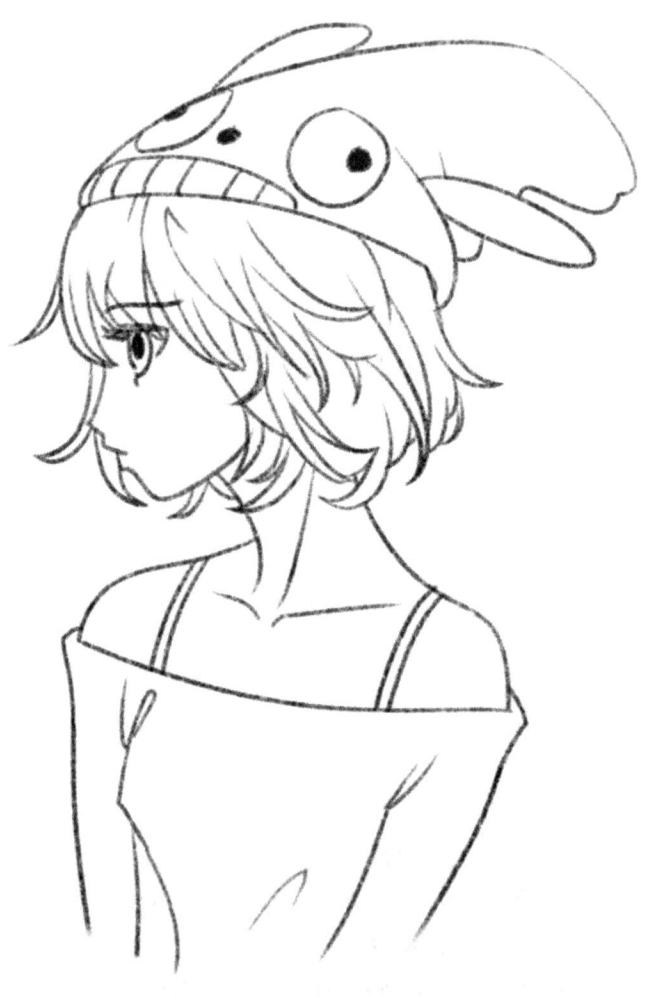

Drawing shape

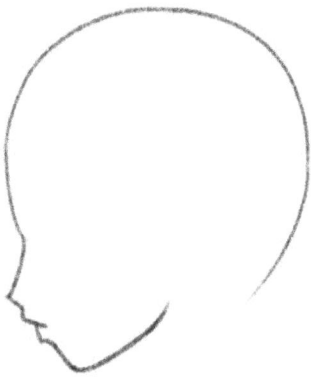

Drawing of cool girl, you will position her so that the outline of her head starts in the middle of the page. Notice the lies that build-up the face and then the angle of the narrow neck. Notice also the tilt of her head down. The placement of the first lines establishes the proportions, so the image is a good size on the page. You get good shapes outside the image, all the white area that is not the image and inside the image, so there I since proportion all around.

Drawing body

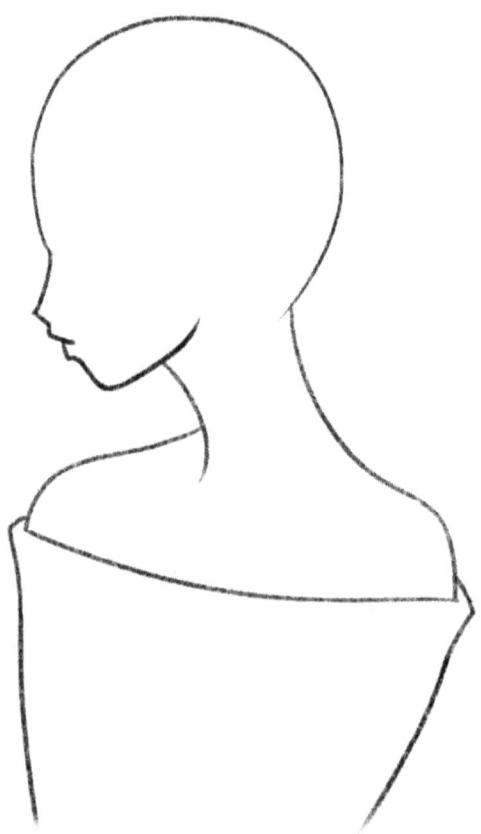

Here it is about sculpting the completed face shape and adding more to the body. Slowly build the face with small lines for each small change in the line. Notice the different angles and directions of the lines. You are also including in this picture the shoulders. See the line of the neck on the left-hand side that extends beyond the line that makes up the shoulder. These small details matter to help create the illusion of what is on the paper.

Draw in the foundation of the eye to help with the placement. Here you see only one side of the optic. Add an apple of the eye, and don't forget to draw the eyebrow. It has thin and elegant form. Sketch some lines to portray the throat and the collarbone.

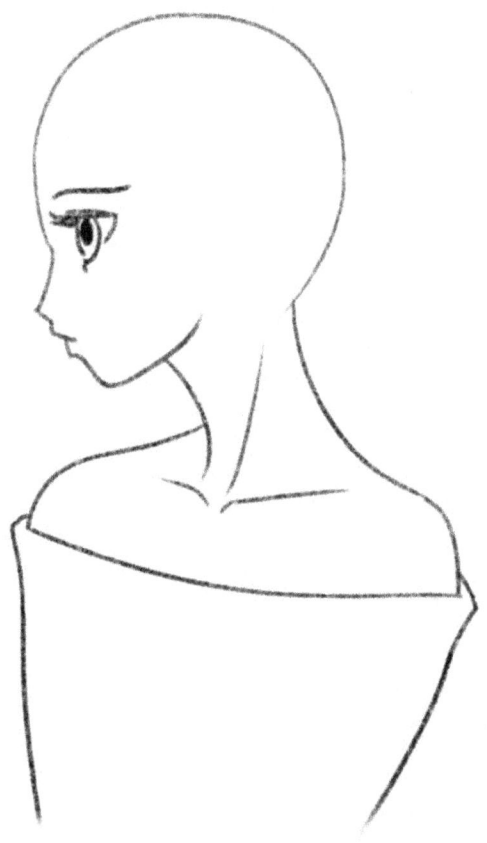

Here you will be drawing in some hair, arms and dress. Create the outer line of the hair, as always notice the curve and direction for it all to look right. Notice the gentle the extensions of the lines and then the curves in different directions on the bottom. The lines of the hair will wave slightly, and they lean to different directions to get the look you want. On her shoulders as well, there are some sweeping grand lines for some contrast and on her blouse. Don't forget to add the beginning lines for the arms.

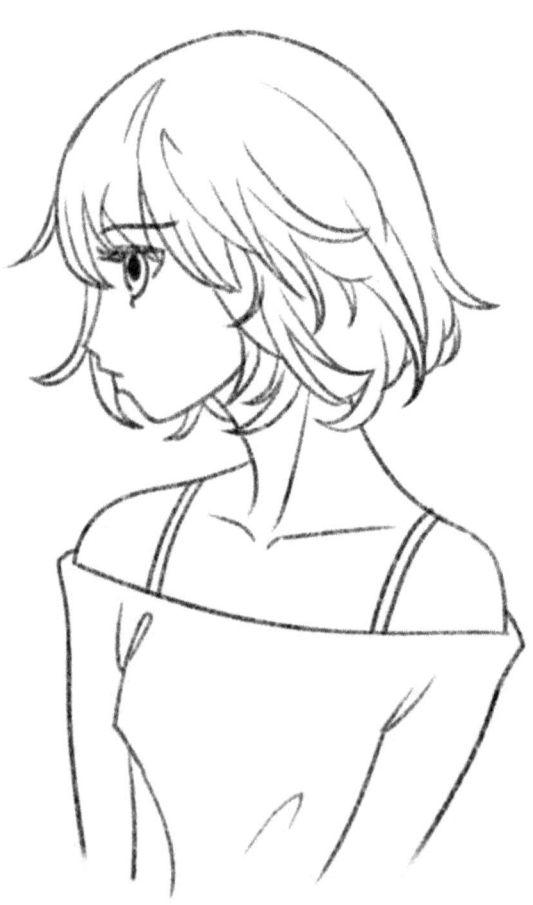

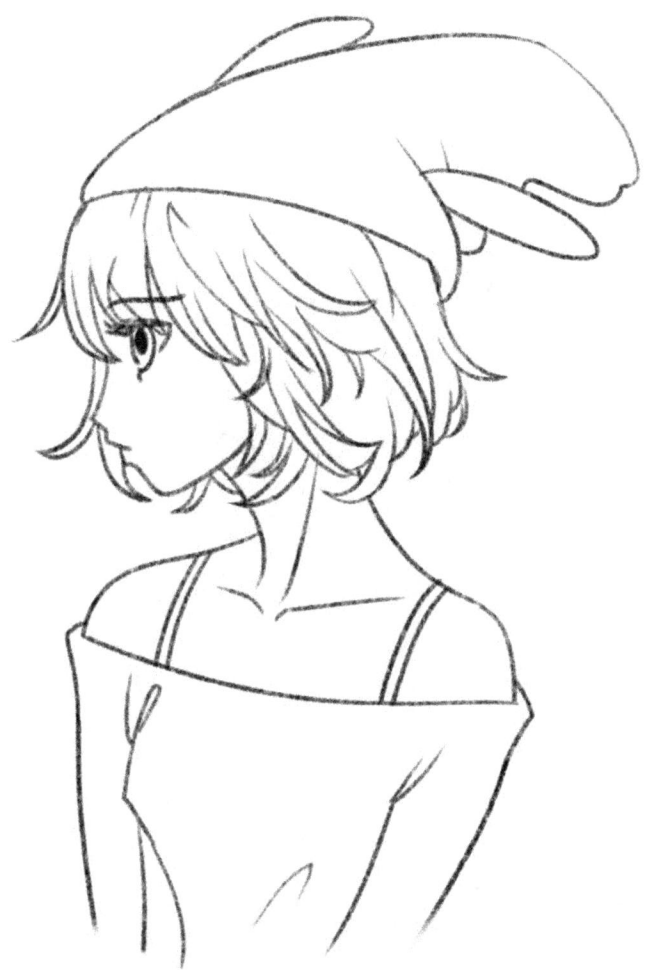

Now it is the time to draw her cool style hat. The hat has ears. It looks like a baggy shape and quite large.

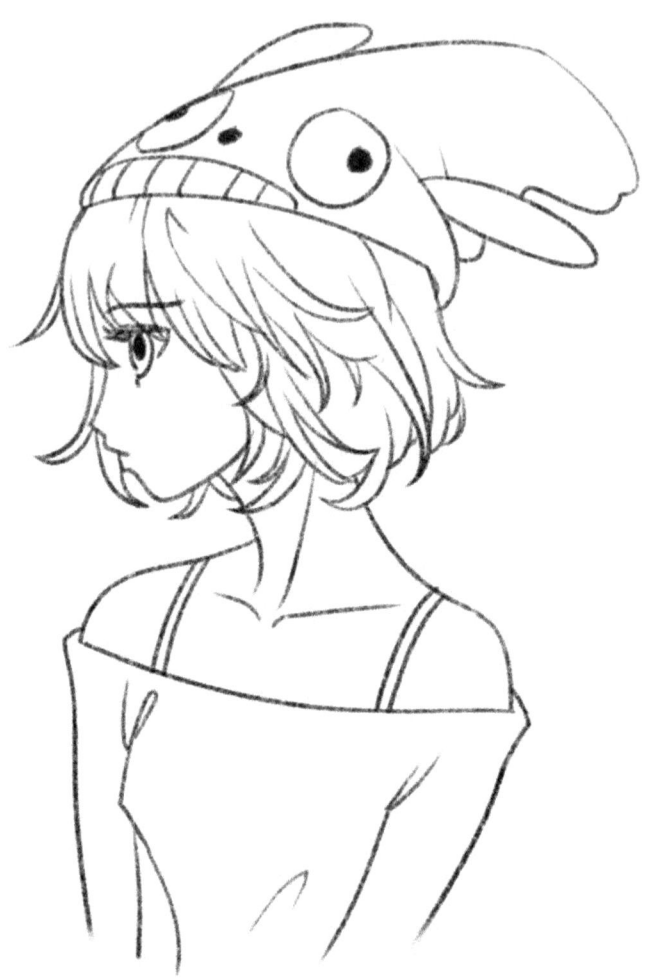

Here you draw an attractive face on her hat. We can see eyes, nose and mouth, it looks like funny and joyfully. Draw eyes larger than nose. The mouth is like the imitation of beaming smile.

Chapter 7 – Funny Cat

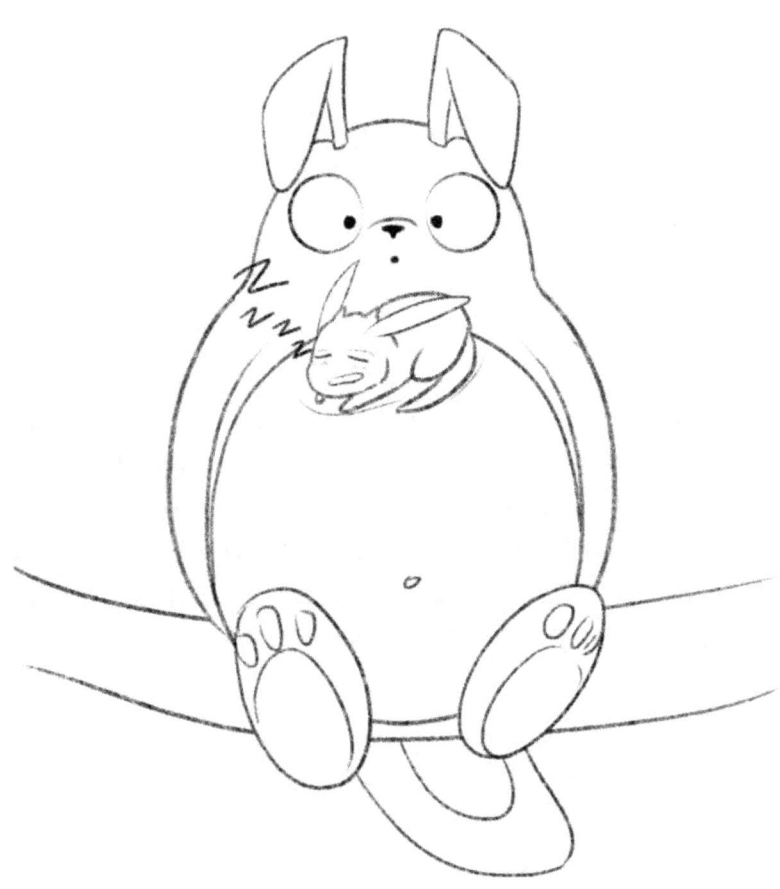

Drawing shape

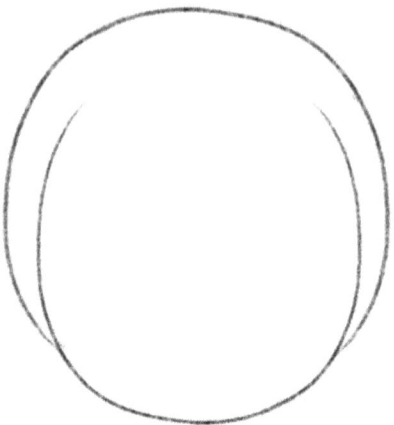

For the first drawing you are going to put your guideline shapes approximately where the anime animal is going to be on the paper. Remember the center is a little to the left of the center it does not have to be perfect, but close. The box shape is going to take up half the page leaving a quarter on either side.

Drawing body

You will start to shape the roundness of the anime animal. You have the size form the box, now put in your wide curves in the bottom boxes and then create the pear shape in the next set of boxes and then the head gourd like in the next box.

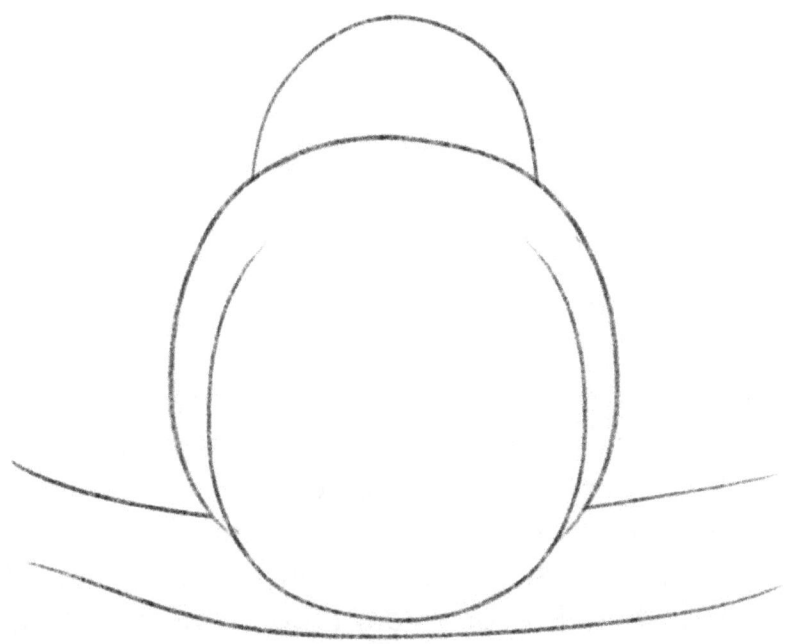

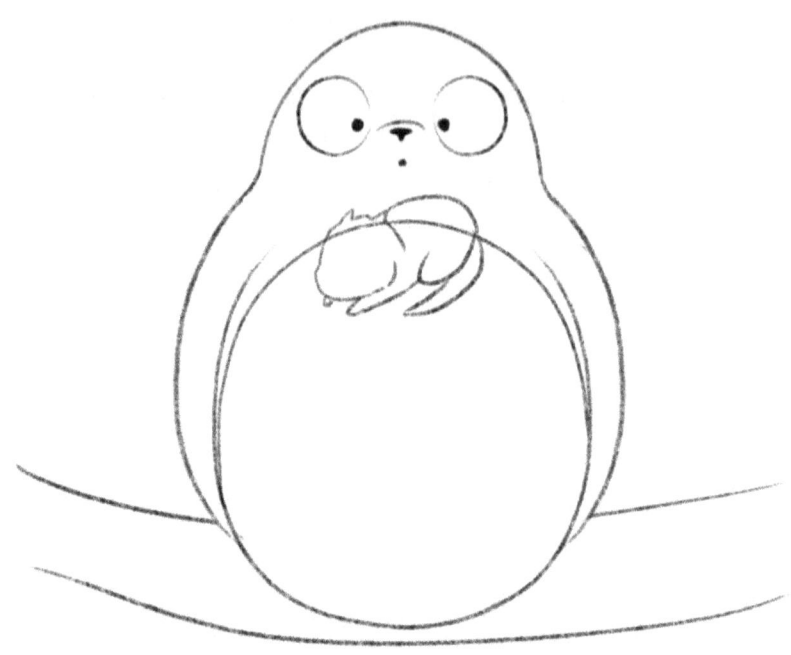

Now it is time to draw the eyes, the nose, and a little more definition to the body. This is the time for the branch to be put in. Notice the bottom of the branch is flush with the bottom of the anime animal. The eyes are scared because we see some animal creature on the cat's belly. There is a lot of definition here so you want to start from the top and put in the little anime animal first. It will be funny pattern!

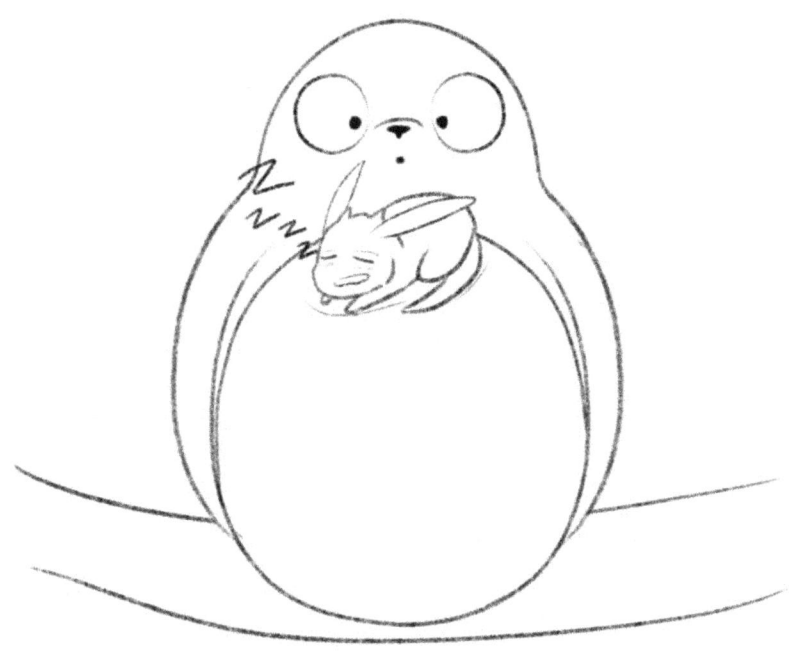

Here anime animal really comes to life. Use the line that breaks up the little animal to position the eyes, nose, long ears and other facial features. Notice this little animal is sleeping. Then look to your picture and draw what is necessary. You can see the difference between this picture and the others, the angles and directions of the features drawn are a little easier.

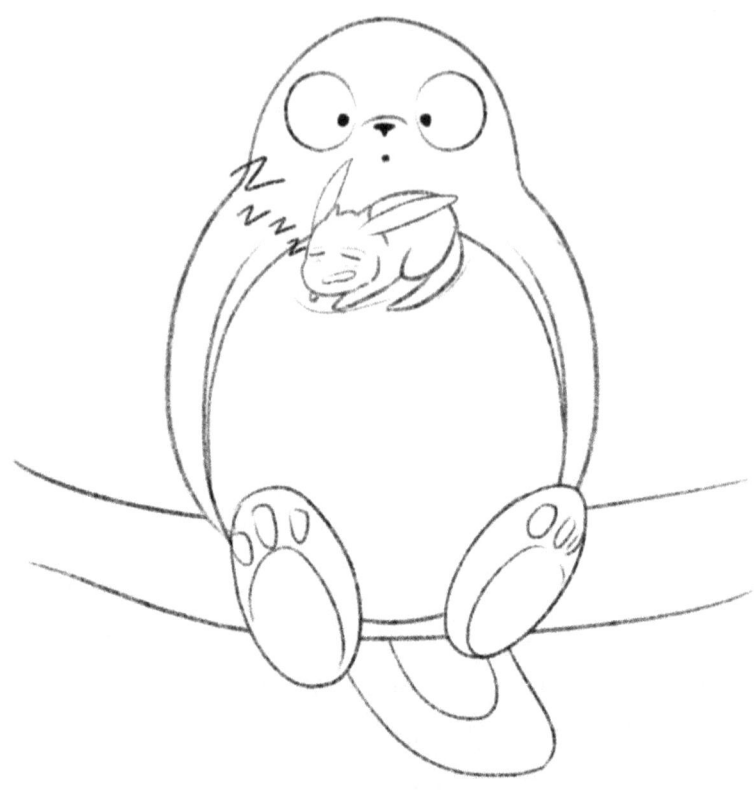

It is about adding a little more detail. As you move down the animal you will draw the tail design and then the little legs with claws. Take note of the ellipses that make up the legs and the angles they are at.

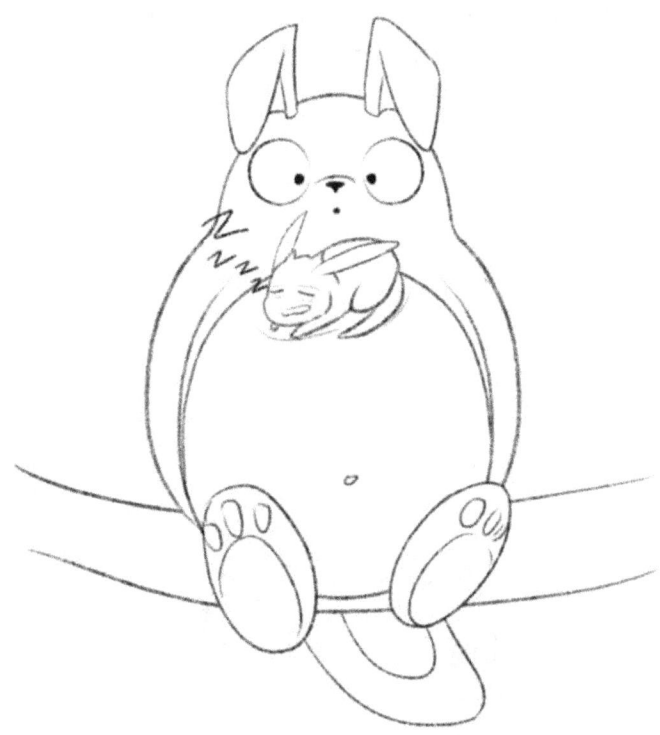

Here you add the ears, they are dangling and it's cute. The squiggles at the bottom of the ears will need to be drawn in. Use the line that breaks up the animal to position the eyes, nose, and other facial features. As you move down the animal you will put in the stomach design and then the little claws, and tail. Don't forget to draw belly button, it gives the real view. Study this picture first before you start so you have an idea of what you are doing. Then look to your picture and draw what is necessary. Erase when necessary. You can see the difference between this picture and the others, the angles and directions of the features drawn are a little easier.

Chapter 8 – Sexy anime girl: learn to draw female body and position

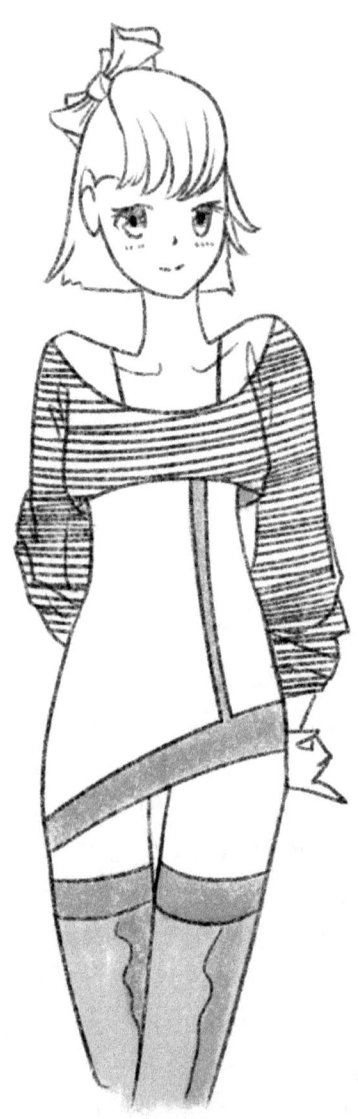

Drawing body

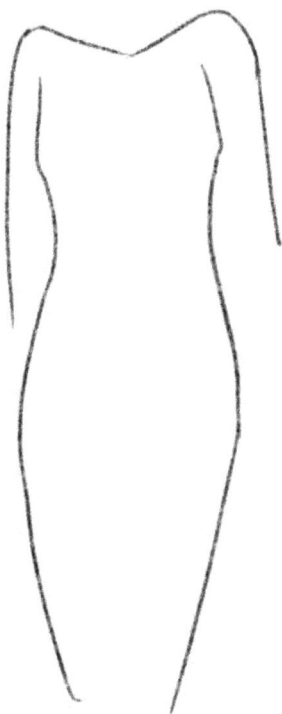

Firstly, girl is getting her outline and shape on the paper. There is the center line you see with the gradual angle and then the line for her legs is straighter yet there is still a slight angle to it.

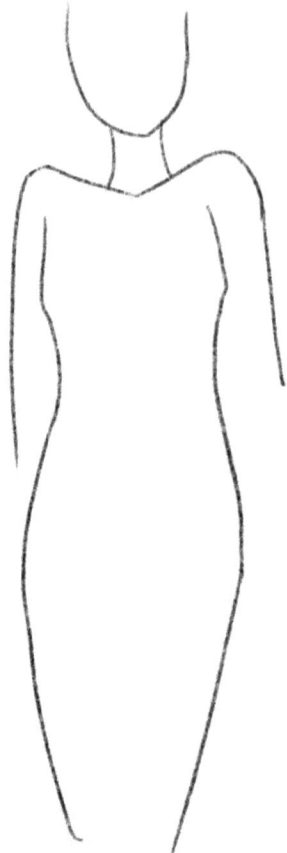

Take a look at the angle of her head and draw the lines
to create her head accordingly.

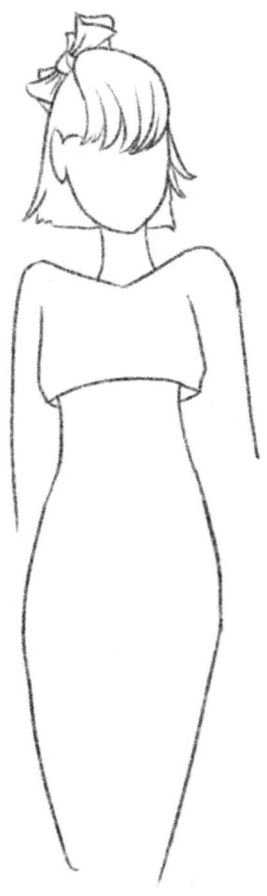

Now is the time for her face and frilly stuff. It is time to draw in the hair and bow. We are back to the different subtle angles with the lines. This is the time to draw her oversized dress taking note the places where the small lines go out and in to make up the detail. This is also the time to draw in her bow. Take a look at this picture then at your own and compare the two adjusting as you go.

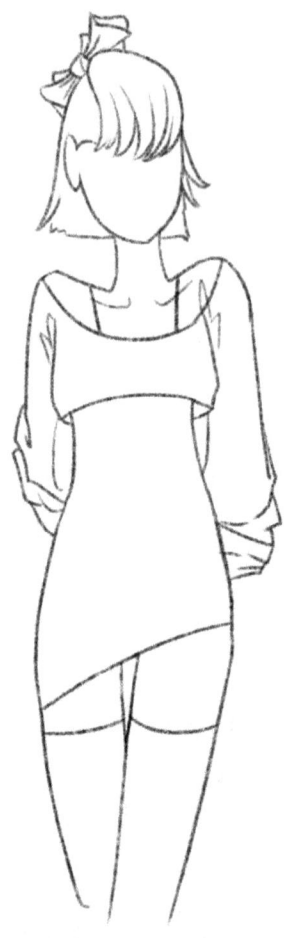

It is the time to add all the shades and shadows to the hair and the folds in the fabric of her dress. Starting from the top of the dress you can sweep across your picture and match all the hatching lines in all the different spots to make sure you get them all in. Notice the shapes that make up the impression of her hand on the right side behind her back. The stockings are simply just a few curved lines.

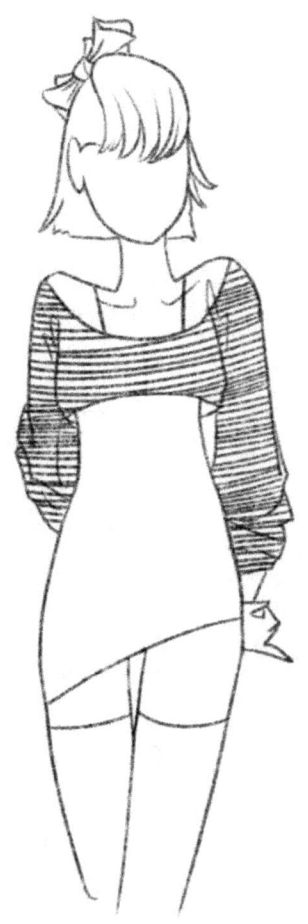

Make sure your guidelines are in place. Then use a fine tipped marker to follow the lines that you set forth for yourself on your paper. Study the frilly of the skirt for a little and see how some lines are the angled ones that appear up and down and some are wavy ones, they are all random. Try to make a swooping confident stroke, but make sure that they are random to make the frills come out as you would like them to. Her stockings just require subtle angled lines.

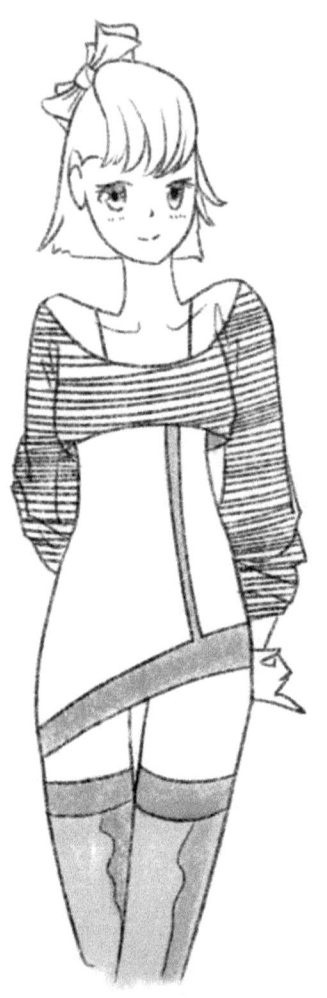

This final step you are completing girl's face. You're drawing big beautiful eyes, small nose and narrow mouth. Take a pen and make the hatching lines that make up the subtle lines of the up dress. Then some cross-hatching lines for shades and shadows. This is a lot of hatching and detail, if you get it at first, fantastic. If you have to draw girl again to get it right no problem, do it however many times you need to get it the way you want.

Conclusion

Drawing anime is fun and exciting. I certainly hope that these seven pictures gave you some insight into the style and ways of anime. If you did not notice there are some very significant details that help make up the anime look. The biggest feature is the eyes. They are the doe like eyes of a young child in almost all anime pictures. They are vibrant full of innocence eyes, full of spirit. The other very significant detail of anime is jagged edges in the hair. The jagged edges in the hair create a very modern look for the subject. There seems to be some sort of cuteness about the overall subjects as well.

As you can see from the beginning of each drawing, having a guideline is of the utmost importance to really get the picture going on the page. It is easy to create a picture that doesn't fill up the page and look like anything interesting. I hope you could see that when you create that mass with shapes you turn out with a very intriguing picture. Besides the shapes, I hope it is apparent that the variety of angles on the lines also helps to make a dynamic picture. The subtle little details in a picture add to its overall great look and wonderful illusion. Drawing is a hobby you can do for the rest of your life. It opens up pathways in your mind that you do not use in your everyday life. There is no limit to what can be drawn. The discovery of new things to draw and mimic in life is really exciting and a lifelong quest for some. The more you draw the more you see about the world around you. It is easy to see very little of life, but when you draw you see so much more.

I hope that drawing these anime pictures has inspired you to draw more.

If your pictures did not come out the way you see them in the book, just keep trying. It takes some time to adjust your mind to seeing in a drawing, if you have not always been drawing. It is a different language and you have to adjust to it. Remember to fill the page. You want your drawing to make a statement and stand out. Thank you so much for reading this book and I hope that you keep drawing, and possibly come up with your own anime pictures.

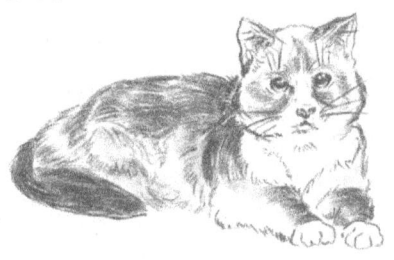

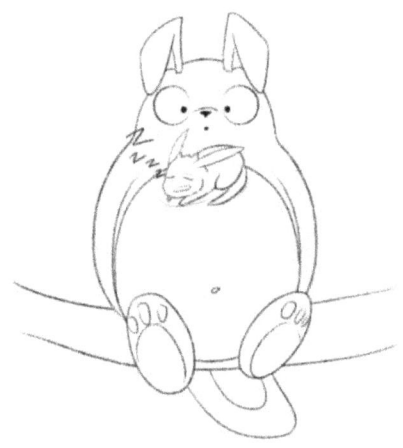

Thank you!

Thanks for choosing my book. If you liked this book, please leave your feedback on **amazon.com**. I'd really appreciate this!
If you would like to have a bonus – **free book** from me, please send the screenshot or the link of your review from amazon.com to this e-mail: gloria.kemer@gmail.com
I'll send you a free book in PDF as a **gift**!

www.ingramcontent.com/pod-product-compliance
Lightning Source LLC
Chambersburg PA
CBHW051223170526
45166CB00005B/2021